Contents

An overview of our books for older, 'catch-up' readers

The Magic Belt, Totem and Talisman 1 & 2 Series are four phonic reading series for older, 'catch-up' pupils. Starting at the very beginning, the reader is swept along with Zak's adventures while learning to read, following step-by-step phonic progression. The table below shows the over-arching structure of the four series and how they interlink.

Series	Suitable for	Reading level	Who is it aimed at?	What does it cover?
Introductory Workbook	Readers aged 8–14	KS1	Absolute beginners. Pupils with shaky knowledge of the sounds and letters of the alphabet, who would benefit from starting a phonics programme from the very beginning	Sounds and letters of the alphabet within CVC words
The Magic Belt reading series (12 books) and workbook	Readers aged 8–14	KS1	Pupils with prior knowledge of the sound and letters of the alphabet	VCC, CVCC, CCVC, CCVCC words and consonant digraphs ch, sh, th, ck, ng, wh, qu, and suffixes –ed and –ing
The Totem reading series (12 books) and workbook	Readers aged 8–14	KS1	Pupils able to read a simple text at CVC level and who know most of the consonant digraphs but have poor knowledge of vowel digraphs	A re-cap of words from CVCC level all the way to CCVCC level and of the consonant digraphs. Introduction of alternative spellings for vowel sounds e.g. the spellings <ai, ay, ai and a> for the sound 'ae'
Talisman 1 Series (10 books) and workbook	Readers aged 8–14	KS1	Pupils who have poor knowledge of the phonic code and alternative spellings for vowel sounds	Re-cap of alternative spellings covered in the Totem Series and additional alternative spellings for new vowel sounds
Talisman 2 Series (10 books) and workbook	Readers aged 8–14	KS1/KS2	Pupils who have gaps in the their knowledge of the phonic code	More complex alternative spellings for vowel and consonant sounds and suffixes

Introduction

This workbook includes six introductory levels which precede the Magic Belt Series. It is a teaching resource aimed at pupils aged 8–14 who would benefit from starting a phonic programme from the very beginning. These pupils may have poor sound/letter correspondences or may be confusing letter names and letter sounds.

The purpose of this workbook is to provide the teacher with materials which will prepare the pupil for reading the Magic Belt Series. The text in the Magic Belt Series starts at CVC[*] and CVCC[**] word level. The activities in the six introductory levels develop the underlying skills for reading: blending, segmenting and phoneme manipulation at CVC word level. They also teach the phonic knowledge needed to read words at this level.

Six chapters introduce the letters of the alphabet and double consonants in a step–by–step progression. Each chapter includes word–building (using the target sounds and letters), spelling, reading accuracy and phoneme manipulation.

Within each level, the pupil can progress from working at single word reading to caption reading and all the way to reading an exciting, decodable, age–appropriate text. Each chapter concludes with a fun reading game to practise and consolidate what has been taught. This progression will build up the pupil's reading skills and confidence. Once the pupil has completed the six levels, he/she will be able to access the text in the Magic Belt Series and activities in the Magic Belt Series workbook.

The levels are cumulative so that the pupils will use previously–taught sound/letters at each level. The phonic progression in these chapters is as follows:

Introductory level	Phonic progression	Word and text level
1	s, a, t, i, m, n, o, p	CVC
2	b, c, g, h	CVC
3	d, e, f, v	CVC/CVCC
4	k, l, r, u	CVC/CVCC
5	j, w, z	CVC/CVCC
6	x, y, ff, ll, ss, zz	CVC/CVCC

[*]CVC = words with a consonant/vowel/consonant structure e.g. 'hat'.

[**]CVCC = words with a consonant/vowel/consonant/consonant structure e.g. 'lost'.

The importance of teaching reading and spelling together

In order for the pupil to understand that spelling (encoding) is a reverse activity of reading (decoding), it is important for the pupil to practise both side by side. For this reason, reading and spelling are taught within each level. Dictation offers the pupil a 'safe' opportunity to spell selected words correctly. This builds up confidence and develops good spelling strategies from the very beginning.

Introductory Workbook

For the
Magic Belt Series

Name: ________________________________

Pupils can use this page as a personalised front cover for their work folder.

Introductory Level 1: s a t i m n o p

Word–building

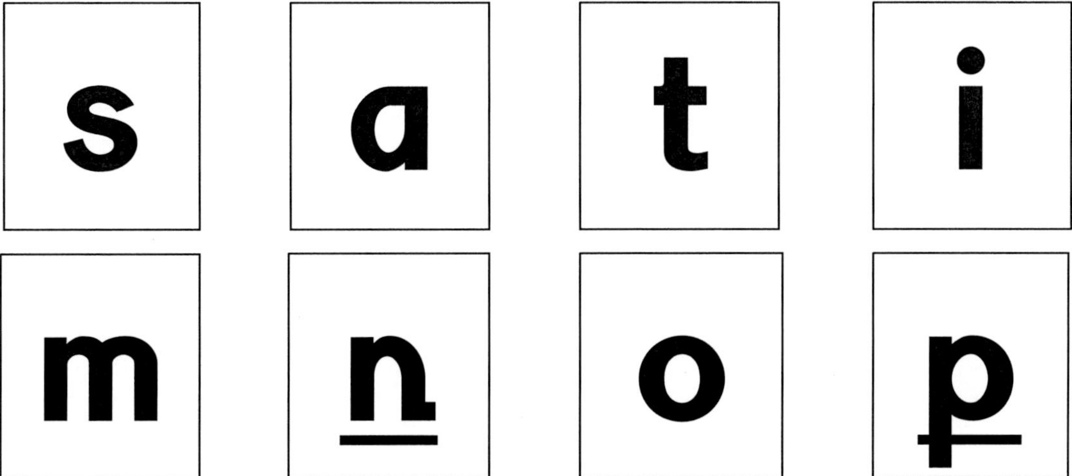

Teaching aims:
- Learn letter/sound correspondences for: s a t i m n o p.
- Segment and blend CVC words with those sounds.

Teacher guidelines:

1. Teach the letter sounds:

Photocopy this page onto card. Cut out the letter cards. Teach the letter sounds. Teach precise pronunciation e.g. 'm' not 'muh'. Keep these cards for use in the next levels.

2. Teach word–building:

Choose a word from the list below. Select only the letters needed to build that word and jumble them up. Draw three lines on a white board. Ask the pupil to build that word by listening to the sounds in the word and segmenting all the sounds in the words one at a time. The pupil then brings down each letter once he/she has segmented the sound in the word. Ask the pupil to read the word he/she has built. Use only two lines if the word has only two sounds.

3. Writing the word:

Ask pupil to write the word on the white board, underneath the lines, saying the sounds as they write the word. He/she then rereads the words he/she has written. Note if the pupil is not forming the letters correctly and teach correct letter formation at another opportunity.

Word list for word–building, reading and spelling:

sat, top, man, at, on, in, pop, nap, not, sip, sin, tip, tin, mat, tot, nit, nip, not, mop, pit, pat, pan

Introductory Level 1: s a t i m n o p

Reading and spelling CVC words

mat	✓
sin	
tip	
nap	
sip	
tan	
nit	
pin	
man	

Teaching aims: Reading and spelling CVC words with the letters: s a t i m n o p

Teaching guidelines: Fold this sheet along the dotted line. Ask the pupil to read the words on the left and tick the words she/he has read correctly. Ask the pupil to turn over the sheet and dictate the words to the pupil. Ask the pupil to spell the words by segmenting and sounding out the sounds as she/he writes them on the lines. Ask the pupil to open the sheet and tick the words she/he has spelled correctly.

Introductory Level 1: s a t i m n o p

Reading accuracy

pat

tap

nip

top

pot

pop

man

nan

nap

pit

tip

pin

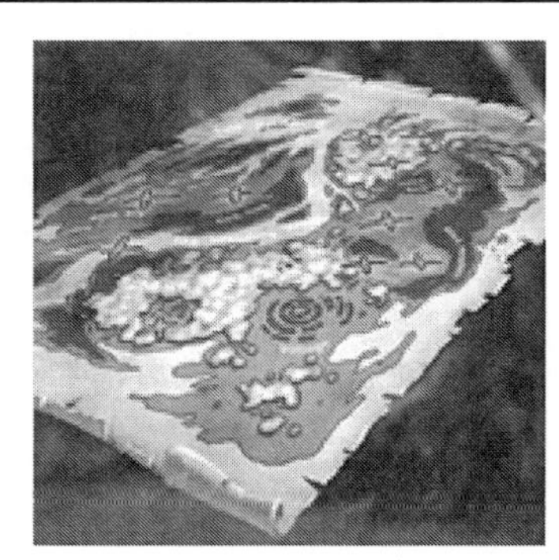

map

mop

Pam

nit

tan

tin

Teaching aims: Reading accuracy

Teaching guidelines: Ask the pupil to read the words in each box and circle the word that matches the picture.

Introductory Level 1: s a t i m n o p

Reading captions

1. <u>Th</u>e tap is on.

2. a tan on a man

3. a pin on a map

4. a nap on a mat

5. a pot and pan

6. a pip in a pot

Teaching aims: Reading captions and comprehension.

Teaching guidelines: Ask the pupil to read the captions and draw a line to the matching picture.

Teaching point: When reading high-frequency words, point to the grapheme the pupil does not yet know and sound it out for the pupil e.g. with the word 'the', sound out 'th' and the shwa sound 'uh'.

Introductory Level 1: s a t i m n o p

Writing captions

1. <u>Th</u> e __ __ __   __ __   __ __.

2. __   __ __ __   __ __   __   __ __ __

3. __   __ __ __   __ __   __   __ __ __

4. __   __ __ __   __ __   __   __ __ __

5. __   __ __ __   __ __ __   __ __ __

6. __   __ __ __   __ __   __   __ __ __

Teaching aims: Writing and spelling captions with CVC words

Guidelines: Dictate the captions from the previous page to the pupil. Ask him/her to listen to the sounds in the words and say them as he/she writes them on the lines.

Introductory Level 1: s a t i m n o p

Full circle game: playing with sounds

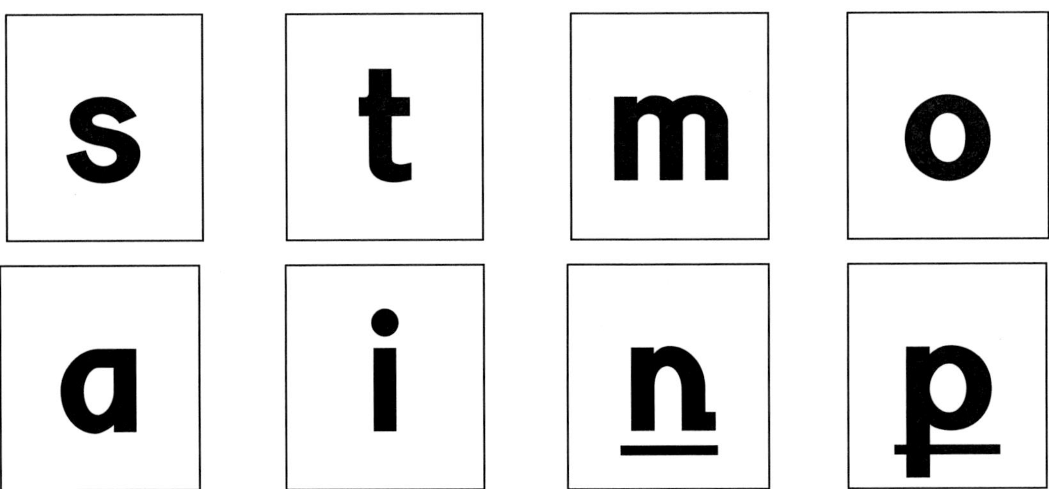

man > mat > pat > sat > sit > sip > tip > nip > nit > not > pot > pit > pin > sin > tin > tan > man

Teaching aims: Practise manipulating sounds within CVC words.

Teaching guidelines: Ask the pupil to build the word 'man'. Explain that you are going to ask him/her to change one sound in the word to make a new word. Ask the pupil to listen carefully to the new word and change the letter of the sound that has changed. Complete the activity until the pupil has returned full circle to the original word 'man'.

The Nap

s, a, t, i, m, n, o, p

Sim has a nap on the mat.

Tap, tap!

"Sit up, Sim!   It is a man!

Sim, it is a man!

Nip the man, Sim!"   Nip!   Nip!

Words the reader may need help with:

has, a, up, the, is

Level 1: Stepping stones game: s, a, t, i, m, n, o, p

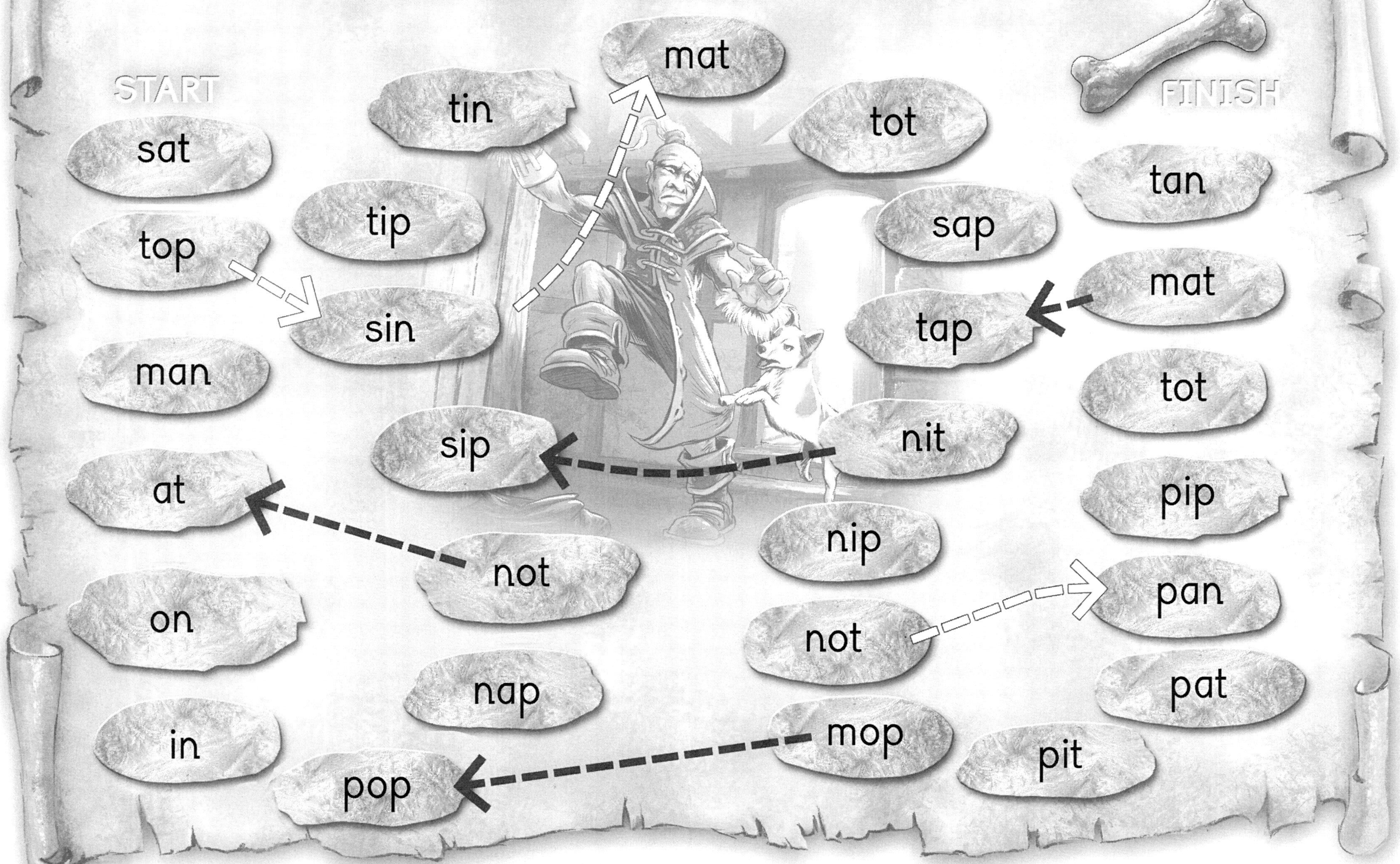

This game is for 1–4 players. Play with counters and die. This sheet may be photocopied by the purchaser. © Phonic Books Ltd. 2012.

Introductory Level 2: b c g h

Word-building

Teaching aims:
- Learn letter/sound correspondences for: b c g h.
- Segment and blend CVC words with those sounds.

Teacher guidelines:

1. Teach the letter sounds:

Photocopy this page onto card. Cut out the letter cards. Teach the letter sounds. Teach precise pronunciation e.g. 'c' not 'cuh'. Keep these cards and add to cards from previous level.

2. Teach word-building:

Choose a word from the list below. Select only the letters needed to build that word and jumble them up. Draw three lines on a white board. Ask the pupil to build that word by listening to the sounds in the word and segmenting all the sounds in the words one at a time. The pupil then brings down each letter once he/she has segmented the sound in the word. Ask the pupil to read the word he/she has built. Use only two lines if the word has only two sounds.

3. Writing the word:

Ask pupil to write the word on the white board, underneath the lines, saying the sounds as they write the word. He/she then rereads the words he/she has written. Note if the pupil is not forming the letters correctly and teach correct letter formation at another opportunity.

Word list for word-building, reading and spelling:

cat, him, got, hat, bin, sag, cop, hog, can, big, hit, ham, hot, bag, cog, cab, hob, nib, tag, bap, bat, tab, sob, mob, hag, gig, gas, bog, gag, bob, bit, bid

Introductory Level 2: b c g h

Reading and spelling CVC words

ham	✓	___ ___ ___	
bin		___ ___ ___	
cap		___ ___ ___	
hob		___ ___ ___	
gig		___ ___ ___	
mob		___ ___ ___	
tag		___ ___ ___	
hit		___ ___ ___	
cog		___ ___ ___	

Teaching aims: Reading and spelling CVC words with the letters: b c g h

Teaching guidelines: Fold this sheet along the dotted line. Ask the pupil to read the words on the left and tick the words she/he has read correctly. Ask the pupil to turn over the sheet and dictate the words to the pupil. Ask the pupil to spell the words by segmenting and sounding out the sounds as she/he writes them on the lines. Ask the pupil to open the sheet and tick the words she/he has spelled correctly.

Introductory Level 2: b c g h

Reading accuracy

bag
big
gap

hit
him
ham

can
cap
cab

bib
bin
nib

cog
cot
cop

not
mob
not

Teaching aims: Reading accuracy

Teaching guidelines: Ask the pupil to read the words in each box and circle the word that matches the picture.

Introductory Level 2: b c g h

Reading captions

1. a bib on a tot

2. cod in a pan

3. a bat in a bag

4. a tag on a cap

5. a cat in a bin

6. ham in a bap

Teaching aims: Reading captions and comprehension.

Teaching guidelines: Ask the pupil to read the captions and draw a line to the matching picture.

Teaching point: When reading high-frequency words, point to the grapheme the pupil does not yet know and sound it out for the pupil e.g. with the word 'the', sound out 'th' and the shwa sound 'uh'.

Introductory Level 2: b c g h

Writing captions

1. __   __ __ __   __ __   __   __ __ __

2. __ __ __   __ __   __   __ __ __

3. __   __ __ __   __ __   __   __ __ __

4. __   __ __ __   __ __ __   __   __ __ __

5. __   __ __ __   __ __   __   __ __ __

6. __ __ __   __ __   __   __ __ __

Teaching aims: Writing and spelling captions with CVC words.

Guidelines: Dictate the captions from the previous page to the pupil. Ask him/her to listen to the sounds in the words and say them as he/she writes them on the lines.

Introductory level 2: b c g h

Full circle game: playing with sounds

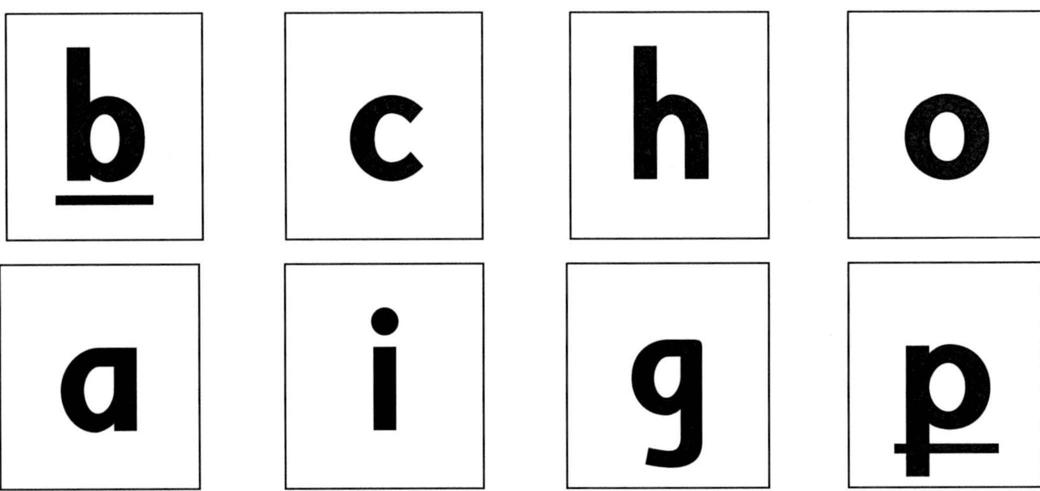

cab > cob > hob > gob > gab > gap > bap > bop > bog > big > bag > hag > hog > hop > cop > cap > cab

Teaching aims: Practise manipulating sounds in words.

Teaching guidelines: Ask the pupil to build the word 'cab'. Explain that you are going to ask them to change one sound in the word to make a new word. Ask the pupil to listen carefully to the new word and change the letter of the sound that has changed. Complete the activity until the pupil has returned to the original word 'cab'.

Introductory Level 2: Decodable text

Hot Dog

b, c, g, h

A big ham.

"I can get the ham.

I can tip the pot!

It is a big ham. I can get it!"

Sim got the ham.

It is hot!

Sim is a hot dog.

Words the reader may need help with:
A, I, the, is

Level 2: Stepping stones game: b, c, g, h

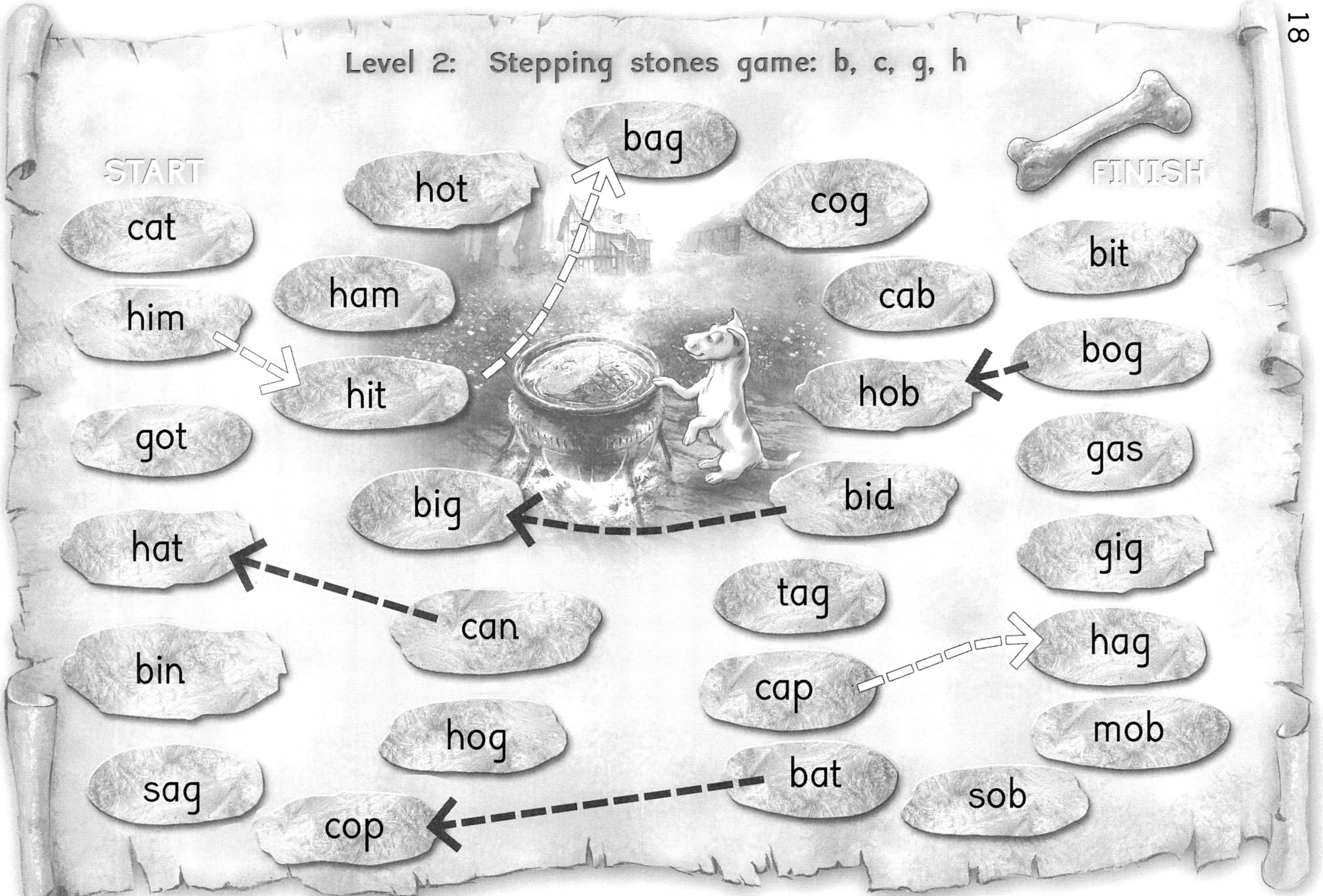

This game is for 1–4 players. Play with counters and die. This sheet may be photocopied by the purchaser. © Phonic Books Ltd. 2012.

Introductory Level 3: d e f v

Word-building

Teaching aims:
  - Learn letter/sound correspondences for: d e f v.
  - Segment and blend CVC words with those sounds.

Teacher guidelines:

1. Teach the letter sounds:

Photocopy this page onto card. Cut out the letter cards. Teach the letter sounds. Teach precise pronunciation e.g. 'f' not 'fuh'. Keep these cards and add to cards from previous levels.

2. Teach word-building:

Choose a word from the list below. Select only the letters needed to build that word and jumble them up. Draw three lines on a white board. Ask the pupil to build that word by listening to the sounds in the word and segmenting all the sounds in the words one at a time. The pupil then brings down each letter once he/she has segmented the sound in the word. Ask the pupil to read the word he/she has built. Use only two lines if the word has only two sounds.

 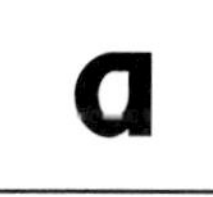 

3. Writing the word:

Ask pupil to write the word on the white board, underneath the lines, saying the sounds as they write the word. He/she then rereads the words he/she has written. Note if the pupil is not forming the letters correctly and teach correct letter formation at another opportunity.

Word list for word-building, reading and spelling:

fan, get, bad, fog, men, dad, met, van, vet, pet, dog, did, dig, got, pen, ten, had, him, mad, dim, fat, dot, peg, net, set, hid, hem, cod, pad, nod, if, hip, fed, fit, god, hen, bed

Introductory Level 3: d e f v

Reading and spelling CVC words

pet	✓		___ ___ ___	
bad			___ ___ ___	
fin			___ ___ ___	
vet			___ ___ ___	
fog			___ ___ ___	
dim			___ ___ ___	
van			___ ___ ___	
fed			___ ___ ___	
dot			___ ___ ___	

Teaching aims: Reading and spelling CVC words with the letters: d e f v

Teaching guidelines: Fold this sheet along the dotted line. Ask the pupil to read the words on the left and tick the words she/he has read correctly. Ask the pupil to turn over the sheet and dictate the words to the pupil. Ask the pupil to spell the words by segmenting and sounding out the sounds as she/he writes them on the lines. Ask the pupil to open the sheet and tick the words she/he has spelled correctly.

Introductory Level 3: d e f v

Reading accuracy

dad
bed
beg

vet
fed
van

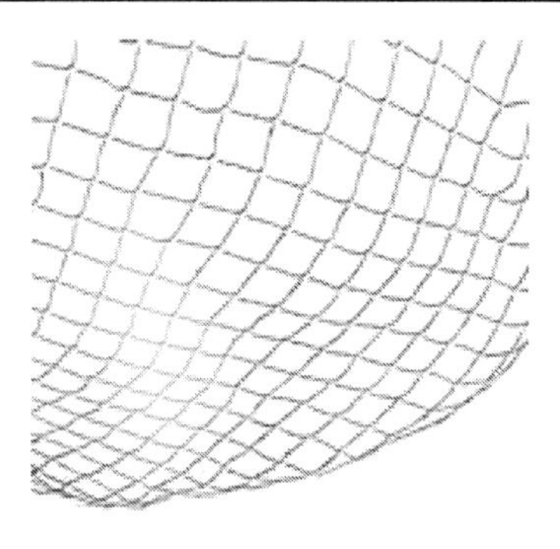

net
met
men

fib
fin
fan

hem
hen
him

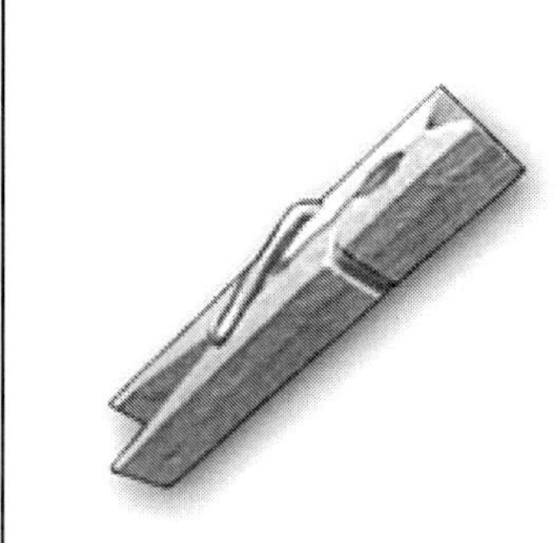

peg
pin
pen

Teaching aims: Reading accuracy

Teaching guidelines: Ask the pupil to read the words in each box and circle the word that matches the picture.

Introductory Level 3: d e f v

Reading captions

1. a pet on a mat

2. a peg and a cap

3. a van in <u>the</u> fog

4. a hen in a pen

5. <u>The</u> fan is on.

6. cod in a net

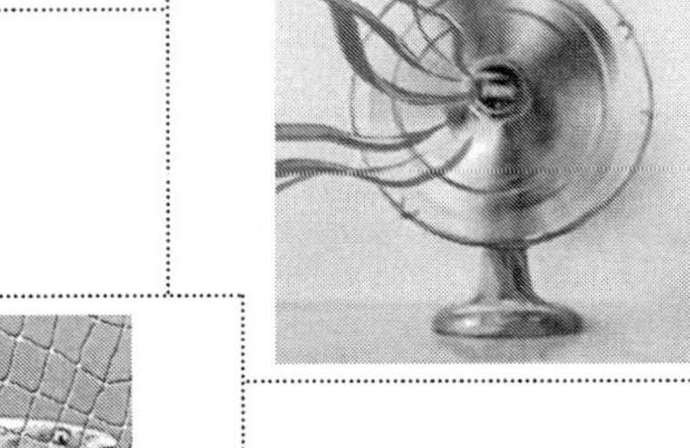

Teaching aims: Reading captions and comprehension.

Teaching guidelines: Ask the pupil to read the captions and draw a line to the matching picture.

Teaching point: When reading high-frequency words, point to the grapheme the pupil does not yet know and sound it out for the pupil e.g. with the word 'the', sound out 'th' and the shwa sound 'uh'.

Introductory Level 3: d e f v

Writing captions

1. __   __ __ __   __ __   __   __ __ __

2. __   __ __ __   __ __ __   __   __ __ __

3. __   __ __ __   __ __   <u>the</u>   __ __ __

4. __   __ __ __   __ __   __   __ __ __

5. <u>The</u>   __ __ __   __ __   __ __.

6. __ __ __   __ __   __   __ __ __

Teaching aims: Writing and spelling captions with CVC words.

Guidelines: Dictate the captions from the previous page to the pupil. Ask him/her to listen to the sounds in the words and say them as he/she writes them on the lines.

Introductory level 3: d e f v

Full circle game: playing with sounds

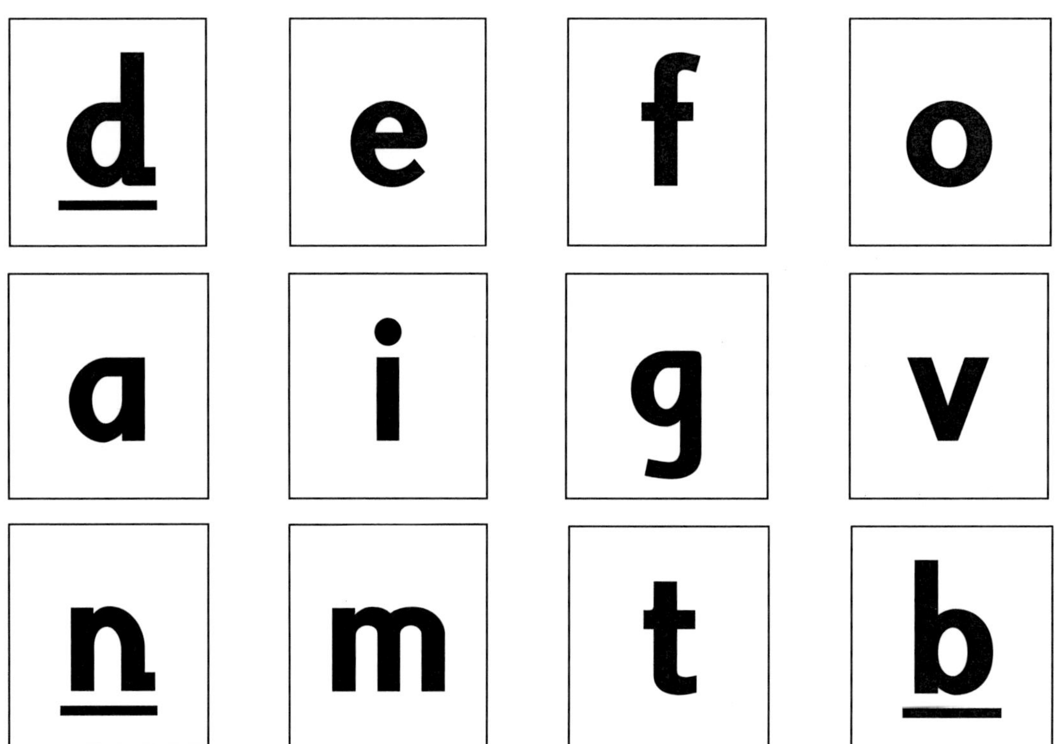

bet > vet > vat > van > ban > bad > fad > fed >
bed > beg > big > bin > fin > din > dig > dog >
fog > fig > fib > fab > fan > man > men > met >
bet

Teaching aims: Practise manipulating sounds in words.

Teaching guidelines: Ask the pupil to build the word 'bet'. Explain that you are going to ask them to change one sound in the word to make a new word. Ask the pupil to listen carefully to the new word and change the letter of the sound that has changed. Complete the activity until the pupil has returned to the original word 'bet'.

Introductory Level 3: Decodable text

Zak Sets Off

d, e, f, v

Zak is fed up.

He has to get up.

He gets the nag. He gets the wagon.

Zak gets the hens in the wagon.

"Hop in, Sim! Get on!"

Zak and Sim set off.

A bad man is in the fog …

Words the reader may need help with:
Zak, is, up, he, has, to, the, wagon, off

Level 3:   Stepping stones game: d, e, f, v

Introductory Level 4: k l r u

Word-building

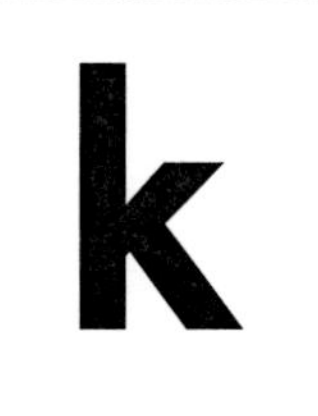   

Teaching aims:
- Learn letter/sound correspondences for: k l r u.
- Segment and blend CVC words with those sounds.

Teacher guidelines:

1. Teach the letter sounds:

Photocopy this page onto card. Cut out the letter cards. Teach the letter sounds. Teach precise pronunciation e.g. 'l' not 'luh'. Keep these cards and add to cards from previous levels.

2. Teach word-building:

Choose a word from the list below. Select only the letters needed to build that word and jumble them up. Draw three lines on a white board. Ask the pupil to build that word by listening to the sounds in the word and segmenting all the sounds in the words one at a time. The pupil then brings down each letter once he/she has segmented the sound in the word. Ask the pupil to read the word he/she has built. Use only two lines if the word has only two sounds.

s u n

3. Writing the word:

Ask pupil to write the word on the white board, underneath the lines, saying the sounds as they write the word. He/she then rereads the words he/she has written. Note if the pupil is not forming the letters correctly and teach correct letter formation at another opportunity.

Word list for word-building, reading and spelling:

sun, up, us, sum, run, rob, bug, bus, cut, gum, hut, mug, mum, pup, ran, log, lot, fig, kit, rag, cup, keg, hum, rat, red, tug, rod, rib, pal, nut, fun, kid, led, let, mud, nil, tub, hub, rip

Introductory Level 4: k l r u

Reading and spelling CVC words

hum	✓		
leg			
ran			
kit			
tub			
rig			
keg			
lad			
rub			

Teaching aims: Reading and spelling CVC words with the letters: k l r u

Teaching guidelines: Fold this sheet along the dotted line. Ask the pupil to read the words on the left and tick the words she/he has read correctly. Ask the pupil to turn over the sheet and dictate the words to the pupil. Ask the pupil to spell the words by segmenting and sounding out the sounds as she/he writes them on the lines. Ask the pupil to open the sheet and tick the words she/he has spelled correctly.

Introductory Level 4: k l r u

Reading accuracy

bus
bud
bug

cub
cup
cut

gum
fan
fun

hum
ham
hut

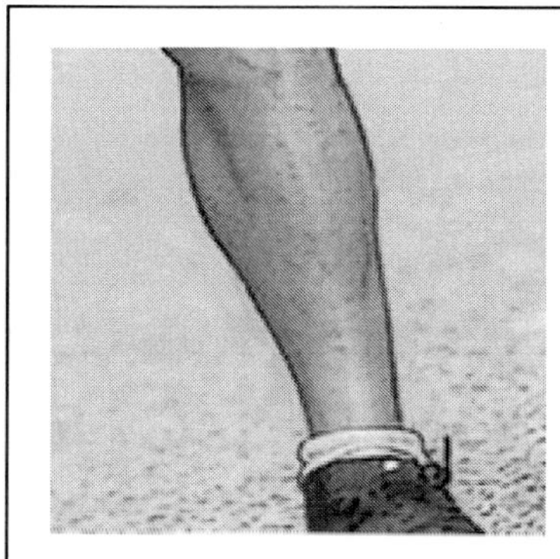

leg
lit
let

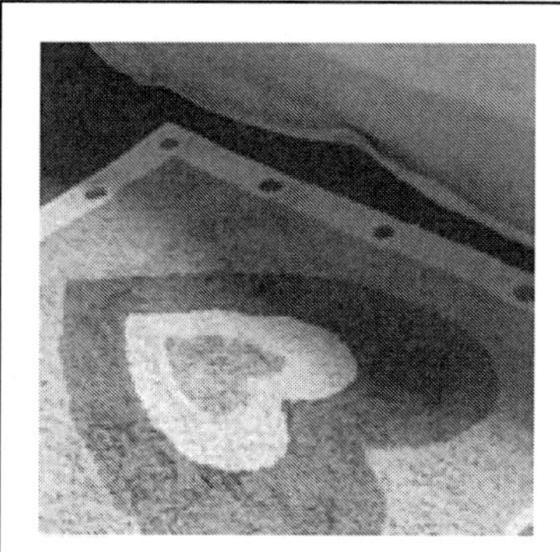

rum
rug
run

Teaching aims: Reading accuracy

Teaching guidelines: Ask the pupil to read the words in each box and circle the word that matches the picture.

Introductory Level 4: k l r u

Reading captions

1. a hut in <u>the</u> sun

2. a sum on a pad

3. a cut on a leg

4. mud on <u>the</u> rug

5. a rat in a cup

6. a bug on a bud

Teaching aims: Reading captions and comprehension.

Teaching guidelines: Ask the pupil to read the captions and draw a line to the matching picture.

Teaching point: When reading high-frequency words, point to the grapheme the pupil does not yet know and sound it out for the pupil e.g. with the word 'the', sound out 'th' and the schwa sound 'uh'.

Introductory Level 4: k l r u

Writing captions

1. __   __ __ __   __ __   <u>th</u>e   __ __ __

2. __   __ __ __   __ __   __   __ __ __

3. __   __ __ __   __ __   __   __ __ __

4. __ __ __   __ __   <u>th</u>e   __ __ __

5. __   __ __ __   __ __   __   __ __ __

6. __   __ __ __   __ __   __   __ __ __

Teaching aims: Writing and spelling captions with CVC words.

Guidelines: Dictate the captions from the previous page to the pupil. Ask him/her to listen to the sounds in the words and say them as he/she writes them on the lines.

Introductory level 4: k l r u

Full circle game: playing with sounds

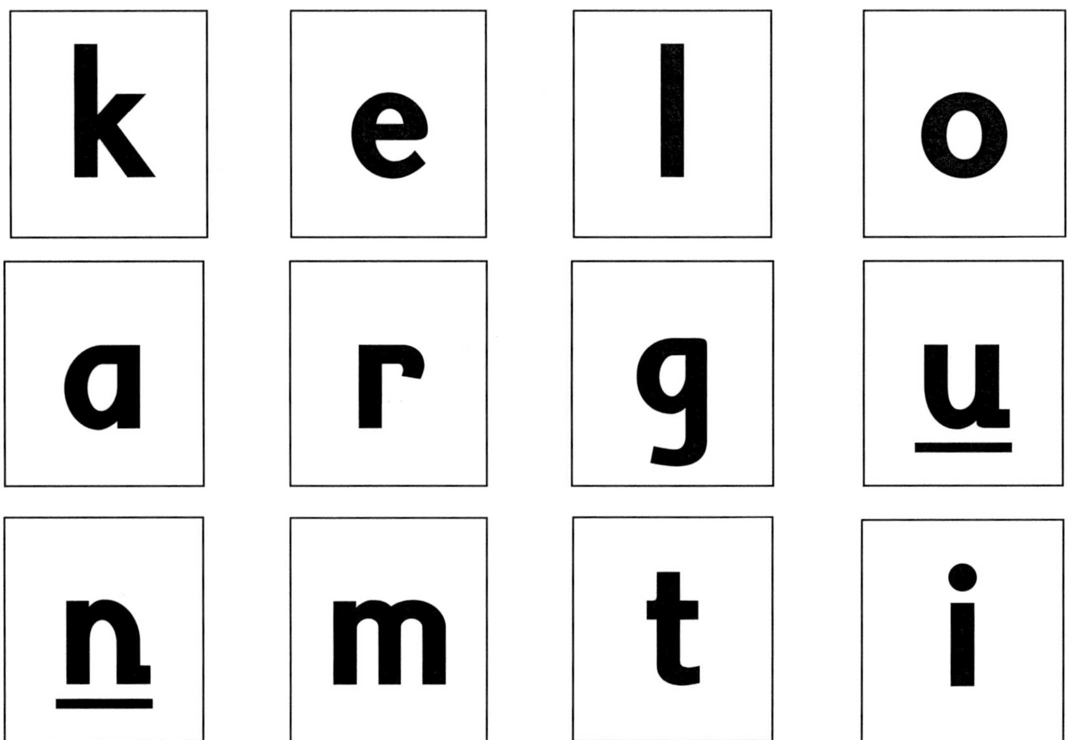

ran > rat > rut > run > rug > mug > tug > lug > leg > log > lot > let > lit > nit > kit > kin > tin > ten > men > man > ran

Teaching aims: Practise manipulating sounds in words.

Teaching guidelines: Ask the pupil to build the word 'ran'. Explain that you are going to ask them to change one sound in the word to make a new word. Ask the pupil to listen carefully to the new word and change the letter of the sound that has changed. Complete the activity until the pupil has returned to the original word 'ran'.

Introductory Level 4: Decodable text

Bad Men

k, l, r, u

The bad men dump a log in the mud.

The nag and the wagon stop.

Sim jumps at the men.

The men hit the dog.

Can the dog get up?

Zak runs.

"Get the kid! Get the lad!"

Words the reader may need help with:
the, a, jumps, Zak

Level 4: Stepping stones game: k, l, r, u

START

sun, up, sum, run, rob, bug

pup, mum, mug, ran, log, cub, fig

hut, gum, rag, cup, hum, rat, kit

tug, rub, red, nut, fun, kid

bus

FINISH

Introductory Level 5: j w z

Word-building

Teaching aims:
- Learn letter/sound correspondences for: j w z.
- Segment and blend CVC words with those sounds.

Teacher guidelines:

1. Teach the letter sounds:

Photocopy this page onto card. Cut out the letter cards. Teach the letter sounds. Teach precise pronunciation e.g. 'z' not 'zuh'. Keep these cards and add to cards from previous levels.

2. Teach word-building:

Choose a word from the list below. Select only the letters needed to build that word and jumble them up. Draw three lines on a white board. Ask the pupil to build that word by listening to the sounds in the word and segmenting all the sounds in the words one at a time. The pupil then brings down each letter once he/she has segmented the sound in the word. Ask the pupil to read the word he/she has built. Use only two lines if the word has only two sounds.

3. Writing the word:

Ask pupil to write the word on the white board, underneath the lines, saying the sounds as they write the word. He/she then rereads the words he/she has written. Note if the pupil is not forming the letters correctly and teach correct letter formation at another opportunity.

Word list for word-building, reading and spelling:

wet, win, jam, jot, wag, web, zip, wed, jut, jog, jet, wig, job, jab, jug, wit, wok, jig

Introductory Level 5: j w z

Reading and spelling CVC words

jam	✓		
wag			
win			
jot			
wet			
jug			
wig			
job			
zip			

Teaching aims: Reading and spelling CVC words with the letters: j w z

Teaching guidelines: Fold this sheet along the dotted line. Ask the pupil to read the words on the left and tick the words she/he has read correctly. Ask the pupil to turn over the sheet and dictate the words to the pupil. Ask the pupil to spell the words by segmenting and sounding out the sounds as she/he writes them on the lines. Ask the pupil to open the sheet and tick the words she/he has spelled correctly.

Introductory Level 5: j w z

Reading accuracy

zip
zap
fez

wet
wed
web

wag
wig
win

jam
jog
jug

wok
win
wet

jig
jet
job

Teaching aims: Reading accuracy

Teaching guidelines: Ask the pupil to read the words in each box and circle the word that matches the picture.

Introductory Level 5: j w z

Reading captions

1. a big win

2. a big, fat jug

3. jam in a bap

4. a wet pet

5. a big web

6. a fun wig

Teaching aims: Reading captions and comprehension.

Teaching guidelines: Ask the pupil to read the captions and draw a line to the matching picture.

Teaching point: When reading high-frequency words, point to the grapheme the pupil does not yet know and sound it out for the pupil e.g. with the word 'the', sound out 'th' and the shwa sound 'uh'.

Introductory Level 5: j w z

Writing captions

1. __ __ __ __ __ __ __

2. __ __ __ __, __ __ __ __ __ __

3. __ __ __ __ __ __ __ __ __

4. __ __ __ __ __ __ __

5. __ __ __ __ __ __ __

6. __ __ __ __ __ __ __

Teaching aims: Writing and spelling captions with CVC words

Guidelines: Dictate the captions from the previous page to the pupil. Ask him/her to listen to the sounds in the words and say them as he/she writes them on the lines.

Introductory level 5: j w z

Full circle game: playing with sounds

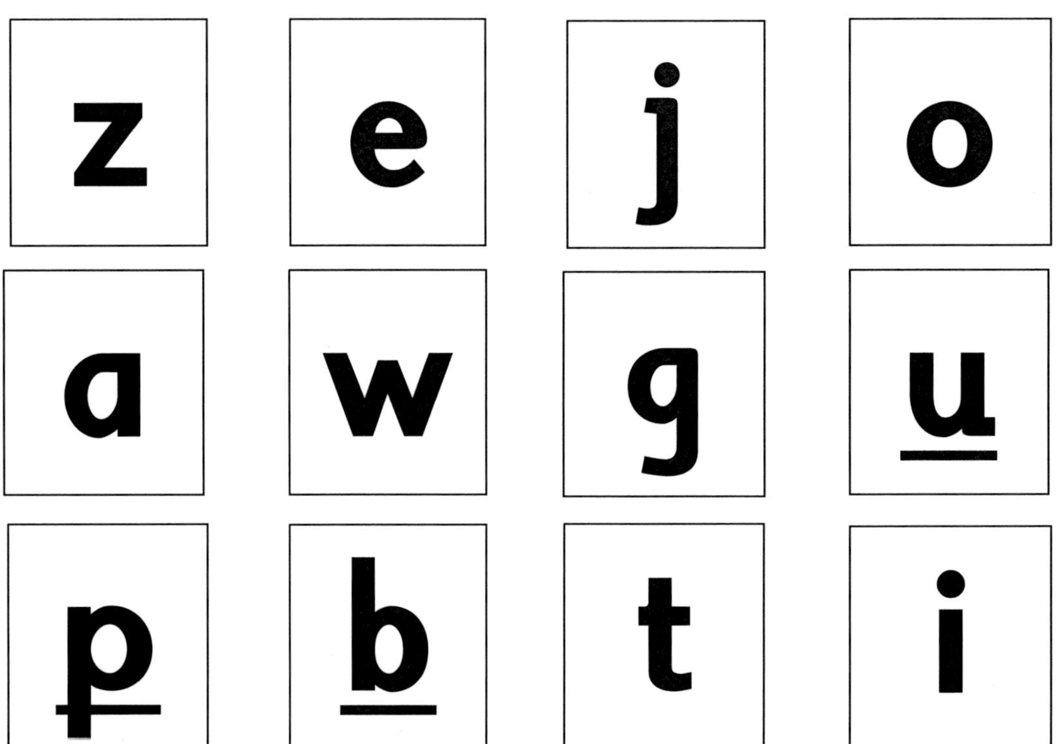

jot > jog > jig > wig > wag > zag > zig > pig >
pug > jug > jut > jet > wet > wit > bit > pit >
pet > bet > get > gut > got > jot

Teaching aims: Practise manipulating sounds in words.

Teaching guidelines: Ask the pupil to build the word 'jot'. Explain that you are going to ask them to change one sound in the word to make a new word. Ask the pupil to listen carefully to the new word and change the letter of the sound that has changed. Complete the activity until the pupil has returned to the original word 'job'.

Introductory Level 5: Decodable text

Bad Jim

j, w, z

Bad Jim hits the dog.

The dog is in the mud.

Bad Jim yanks Zak.

He jabs Zak in the ribs.

"Sit in the wagon!" yells Bad Jim.

"Sim!" yells Zak.

Wag, wag. Sim gets up.

Is it Finn, Zak's pal, next to the wagon?

Words the reader may need help with:
the, is, yanks, he, yells, next

Level 5: Stepping stones game: j, w, z

Introductory Level 6: x y ff ll ss zz

Word-building

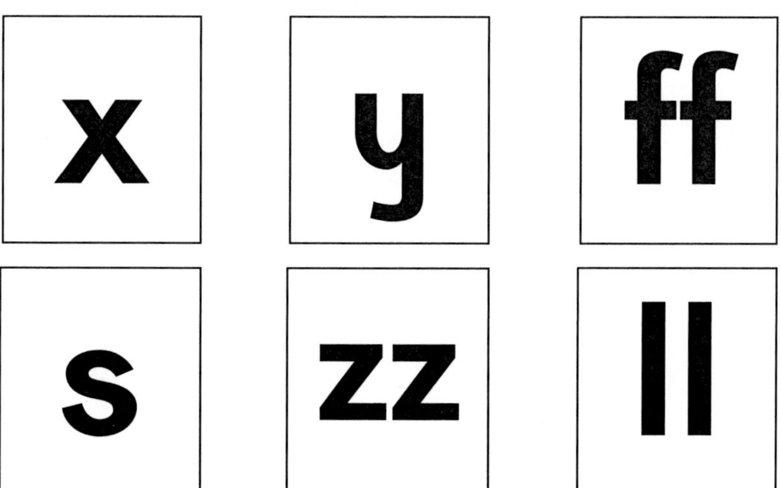

Teaching aims:
- Learn letter/sound correspondences for: x y ff ll ss zz.
- Segment and blend CVC words with those sounds.

Teacher guidelines:

1. Teach the letter sounds:

Photocopy this page onto card. Cut out the letter cards. Teach the letter sounds. Teach precise pronunciation e.g. 'y' not 'yuh'. Keep these cards for use in the next levels.

2. Teach word-building:

Choose a word from the list below. Select only the letters needed to build that word and jumble them up. Draw three lines on a white board. Ask the pupil to build that word by listening to the sounds in the word and segmenting all the sounds in the words one at a time. The pupil then brings down each letter once he/she has segmented the sound in the word. Ask the pupil to read the word he/she has built. Use only two lines if the word has only two sounds.

| b | o | x |

b   *o*   *x*

3. Writing the word:

Ask pupil to write the word on the white board, underneath the lines, saying the sounds as they write the word. He/she then rereads the words he/she has written. Note if the pupil is not forming the letters correctly and teach correct letter formation at another opportunity.

Word list for word-building, reading and spelling:

box, fix, mix, wax, six, tax, yak, yes, yam, yap, yob, yet, off, puff, cuff, bell, fell, kill, boss, fuss, buzz, fizz, jazz, less, will, yell, sell, pill, hill, gull, doll, mess, miss, tell, loss, tiff, till, well

This sheet may be photocopied by the purchaser. © Phonic Books Ltd 2012

Introductory Level 6: x y ff ll ss zz

Reading and spelling CVC words

mix	✓		___ ___ ___	
wax			___ ___ ___	
yes			___ ___ ___	
puff			___ ___ ___ ___	
sell			___ ___ ___ ___	
doll			___ ___ ___ ___	
loss			___ ___ ___ ___	
miss			___ ___ ___ ___	
buzz			___ ___ ___ ___	

Teaching aims: Reading and spelling CVC words with the letters: x y ff ll ss zz

Teaching guidelines: Fold this sheet along the dotted line. Ask the pupil to read the words on the left and tick the words she/he has read correctly. Ask the pupil to turn over the sheet and dictate the words to the pupil. Ask the pupil to spell the words by segmenting and sounding out the sounds as she/he writes them on the lines. Ask the pupil to open the sheet and tick the words she/he has spelled correctly.

Introductory Level 6: x y ff ll ss zz

Reading accuracy

fox
box
six

yes
yam
yak

cuff
huff
puff

bell
doll
bill

mess
hiss
miss

buzz
fuzz
fizz

Teaching aims: Reading accuracy

Teaching guidelines: Ask the pupil to read the words in each box and circle the word that matches the picture.

Introductory Level 6: x y ff ll ss zz

Reading captions

| 1. a big miss |

| 2. a bill and till |

| 3. fizz in a cup |

| 4. a doll and bell |

| 5. yam in a box |

| 6. ten and six |

Teaching aims: Reading captions and comprehension.

Teaching guidelines: Ask the pupil to read the captions and draw a line to the matching picture.

Teaching point: When reading high-frequency words, point to the grapheme the pupil does not yet know and sound it out for the pupil e.g. with the word 'the', sound out 'th' and the shwa sound 'uh'.

Introductory Level 6: x y ff ll ss zz

Writing captions

1. __ __ __ __ __ __ __

2. __ __ __ __ __ __ __ __ __ __

3. __ __ __ __ __ __ __ __ __

4. __ __ __ __ __ __ __ __ __ __

5. __ __ __ __ __ __ __ __ __

6. __ __ __ __ __ __ __ __ __

Teaching aims: Writing and spelling captions with CVC words

Guidelines: Dictate the captions from the previous page to the pupil. Ask him/her to listen to the sounds in the words and say them as he/she writes them on the lines.

Introductory level 6: x y ff ll ss zz

Full circle game: playing with sounds

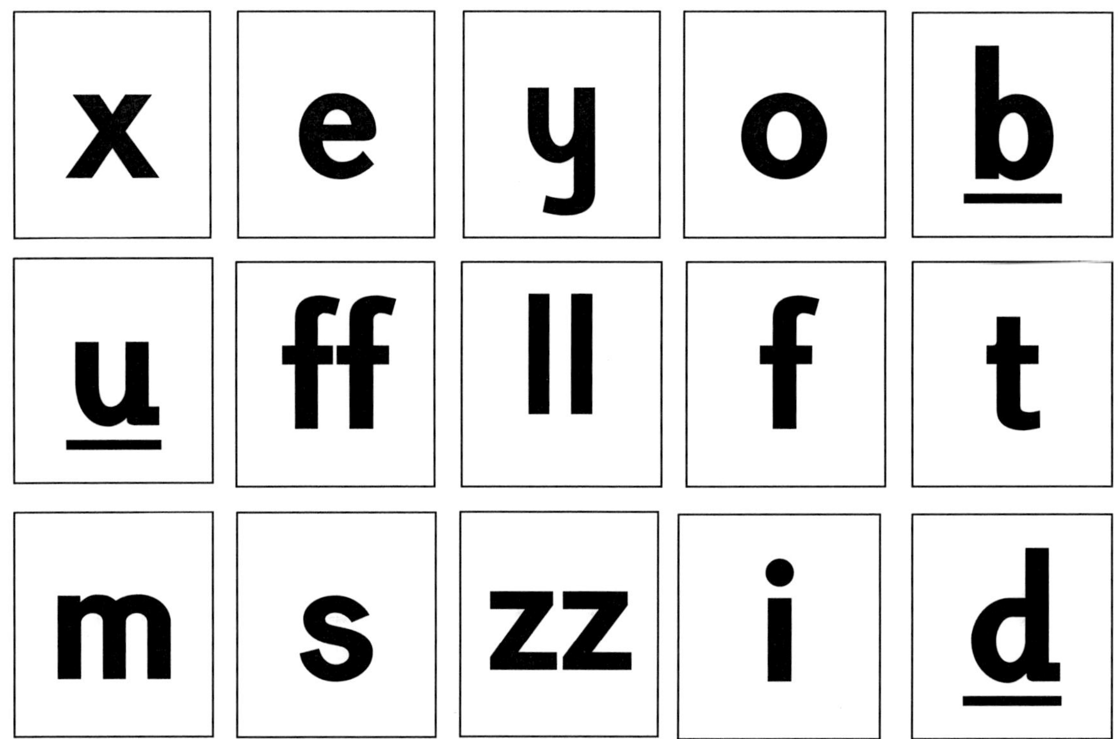

buzz > buff > biff > tiff > till > tell > yell > yet > bet > bell > bess > boss > moss> mess > miss > mix > mill > fill > fix > fizz > fuzz > buzz

Teaching aims: Practise manipulating sounds in words.

Teaching guidelines: Ask the pupil to build the word 'buzz'. Explain that you are going to ask them to change one sound in the word to make a new word. Ask the pupil to listen carefully to the new word and change the letter of the sound that has changed. Complete the activity until the pupil has returned to the original word 'buzz'.

Introductory Level 6: Decodable text

Huff and Puff
`x, y, ff, ll, ss, zz`

Zak runs off.

"Get the kid in the wagon!" yells Bad Jim.

"Yes, boss! OK, boss!"

Finn, Zak's pal, is next to the wagon.

Finn and Zak jump on the nag.

The bad men run but miss the wagon.

The bad men huff and puff.

Words the reader may need help with:
the, OK, is, to,

Level 6: Stepping stones game: x, y, ff, ll, ss, zz

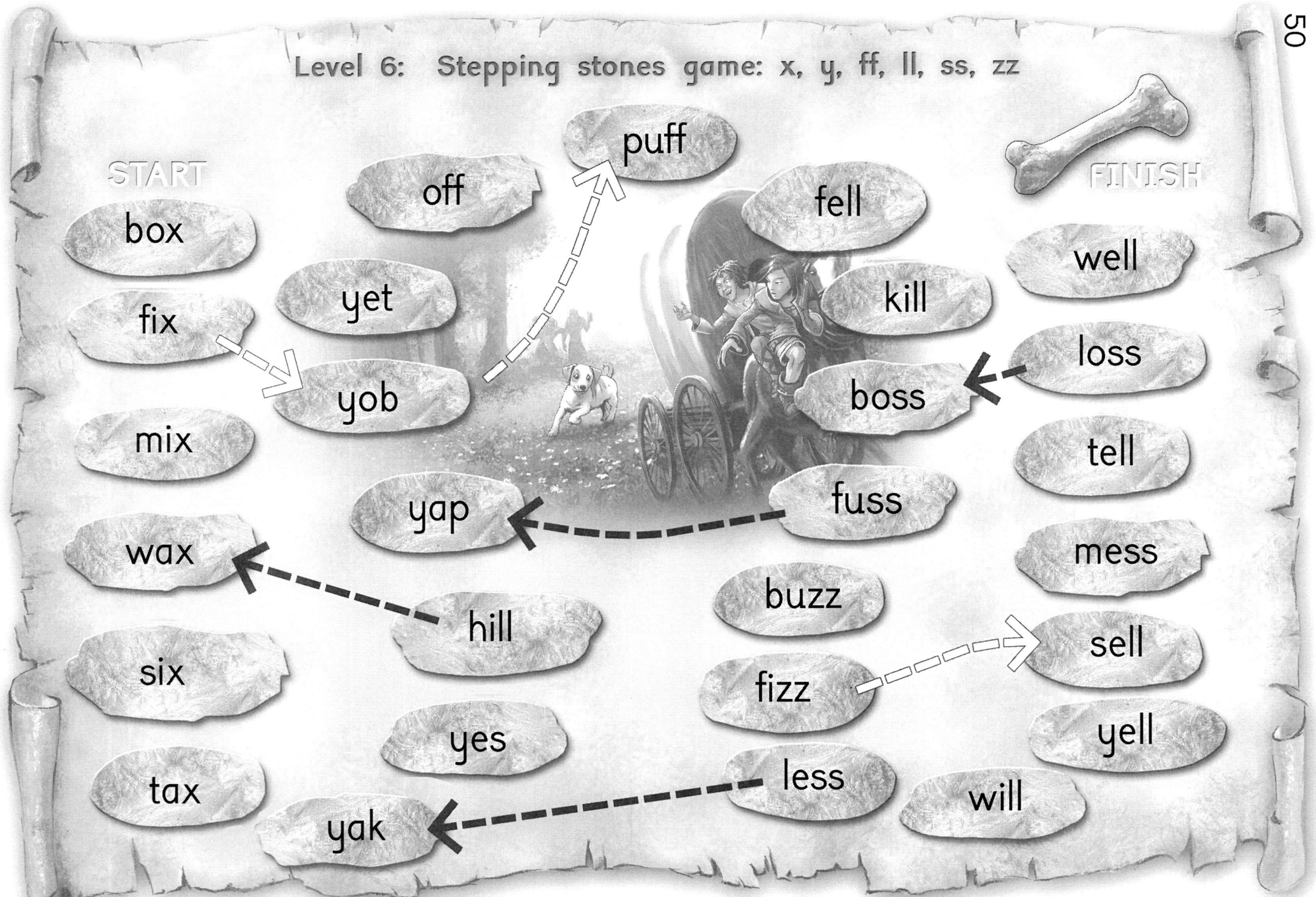

This game is for 1–4 players. Play with counters and die. This sheet may be photocopied by the purchaser.